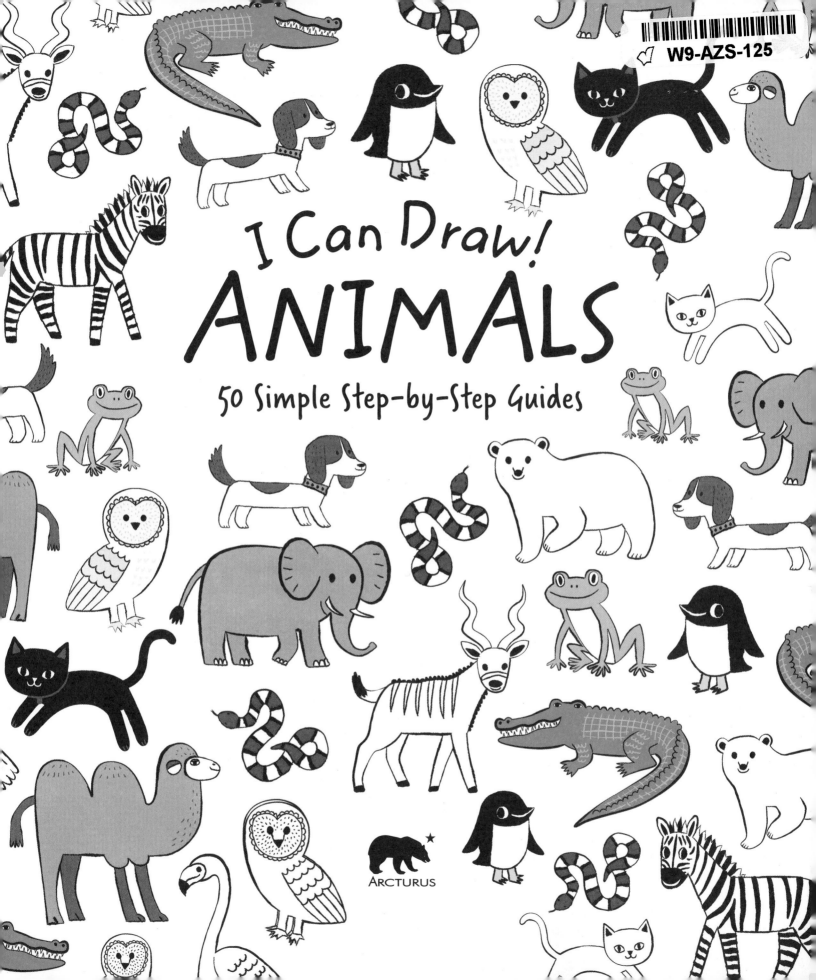

I Can Draw! ANIMALS

50 Simple Step-by-Step Guides

ARCTURUS

ARCTURUS

This edition published in 2021 by Arcturus Publishing Limited
26/27 Bickels Yard, 151–153 Bermondsey Street,
London SE1 3HA

Copyright © Arcturus Holdings Limited

Author: William Potter
Illustrator: Hui Skipp
Editor: Violet Peto
Designer: Stefan Holliland
Managing Editor: Joe Harris

ISBN: 978-1-83940-357-6
CH007806NT
Supplier 29, Date 1120, Print run 10669

Printed in China

CONTENTS

GETTING STARTED

Animals are lots of fun to doodle, with their different body shapes, wings, fins, feathers, and fur. With this book, you can follow simple steps to sketch them as if you were on a spectacular safari. There are also lots of scenes with space for you to draw these animals in their natural homes.

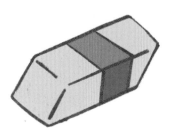

Use a pencil to copy each step and an eraser to erase any mistakes, then go over your lines with a pen. When you're happy with your new animal friends, use paints, pencils, or crayons to fill in the outlines with bright rainbow shades.

Now, turn the page and begin your wild adventure!

CHAPTER 1

PET PARADE

CUTE KITTEN

This young cat is full of life and eager to play.

1

2

3

4

5

6

Which fun fur patterns will you choose?

Mother cat is keeping an eye on her young. Draw her playful kittens having fun.

FUNNY BUNNY

Hop to it and sketch this bouncy bunny.

Here's a hutch for your rabbits to live in.
Draw a pair of bunnies in their new home.

PLAYFUL PUPPY

Time for a walk! Draw a dashing dog, and lead her to the park.

Let the puppies explore the park.
Choose a collar for each to wear.

BIRDIE BUDDIES

This canary and parakeet duo have a song to tweet for you.

Pick a perch for your
new feathered friends.

SCAMPERING HAMSTER

This bundle of fur is ready for some exercise.

1

2

3

4

5

6

7

8

9

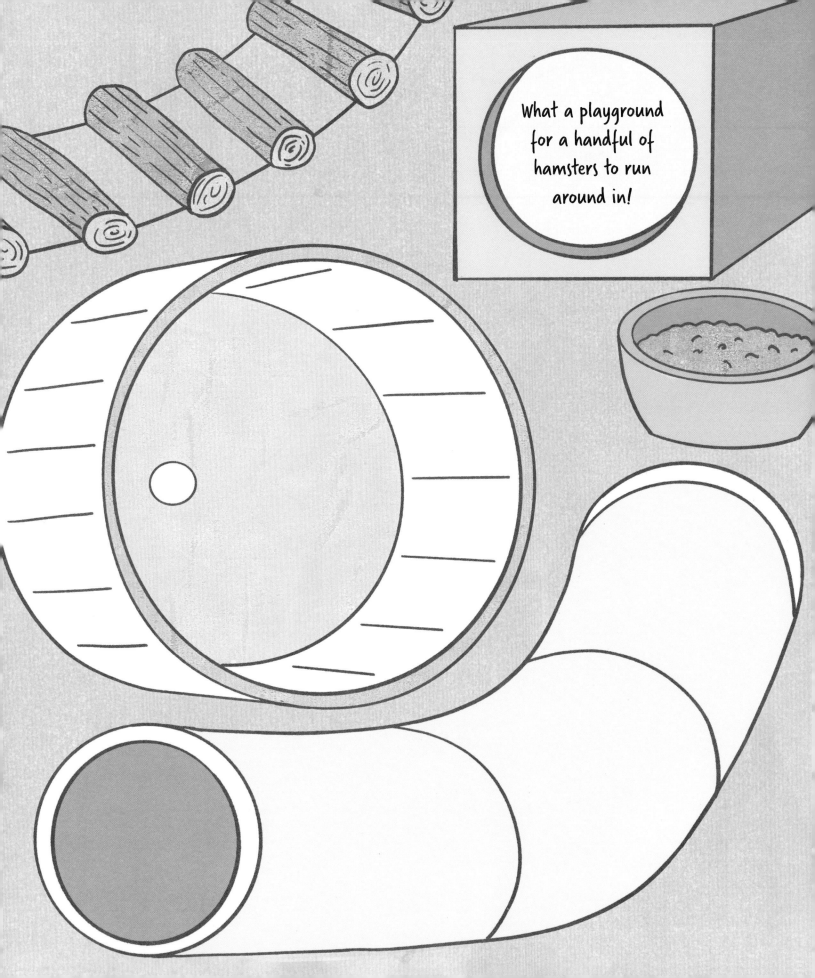

GLITTERING GOLDFISH

Take a dip and draw this bright, shiny fish.

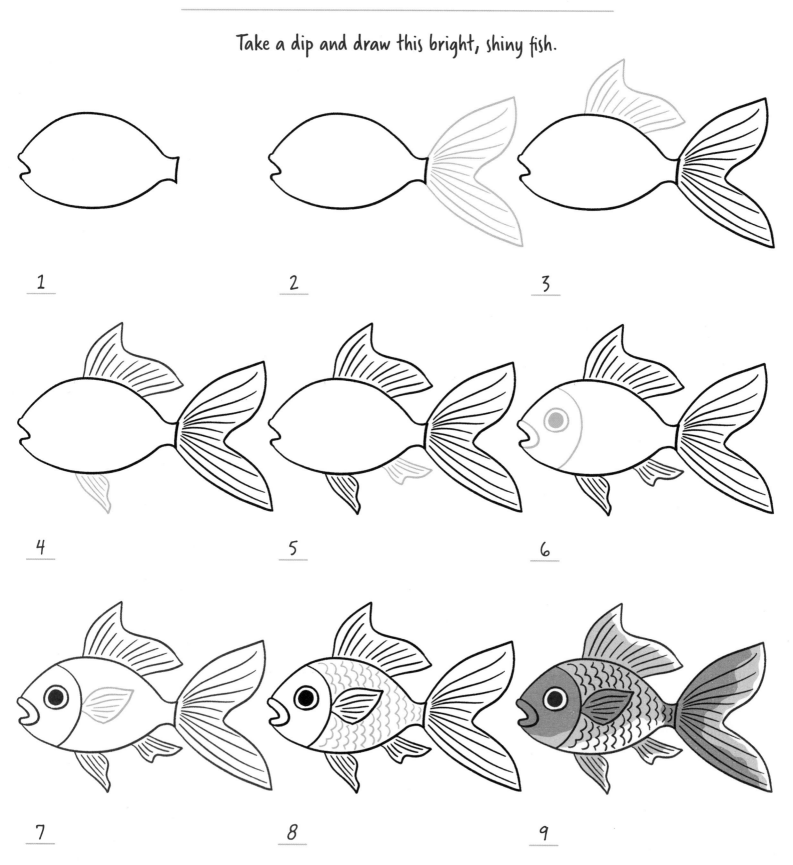

1

2

3

4

5

6

7

8

9

Choose some plants and decorations to keep
your new goldfish happy in their bowl.

MERRY MOUSE

Don't let the cats on page 6 near this little squeaker!

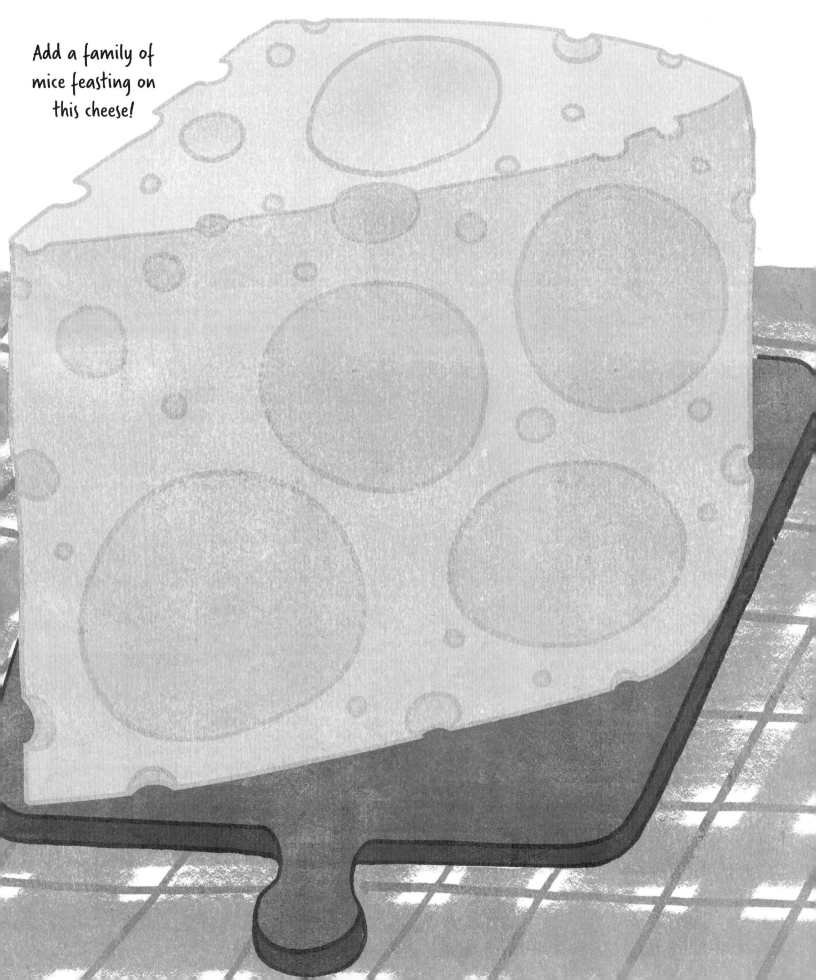

Add a family of mice feasting on this cheese!

Fill this pet store window with lots of different animals to choose from.

CHAPTER 2

DOWN ON THE FARM

CHEERY COW

Get moo-ving ... this cow won't draw itself!

1

2

3

4

5

6

7

8

9

Here's the farmer who has come to lead
the herd to the cowshed for milking.

Give each of your cows a different
pattern of patches.

FLUFFY SHEEP

Once you've mastered drawing a ewe, you can add horns and turn it into a ram.

1

2

3

4

5

6

7

8

9

GRINNING GOAT

A farm with a goat always gets our vote!

1

2

3

4

5

6

7

8

9

PINK PIG

This porker is perfect, right down to its oink!

1

2

3

4

5

6

7

8

9

Pigs love to snuffle in the mud.
Add as many as you can squeeze in.

To add some piglets, just draw the pigs smaller!

HEN AND CHICKS

A mother hen needs some chirping chicks to look after.

Draw some hens roosting in this snug coop. Add some chicks and eggs hatching, too.

DARLING DUCKLING

Make a splash with this delightful young duck.

1

2

3

4

5

6

7

8

9

To show ducklings swimming, you just need to leave out the legs!
Draw some here paddling in the pond.

PRIZE PONY

This pretty pony has won a lot of rosettes in the gymkhana.

Draw your pony on the gymkhana course.

Choose some obstacles for your pony to jump over.

It's the County Fair.
Draw some prize-worthy
animals next
to the farmer.

Give the farmer a trophy to present to the winning animal.

CHAPTER 3

SAFARI TIME

JOLLY GIRAFFE

The world's tallest animal needs some space.

1

2

3

4

5

6

7

8

9

Only a giraffe is tall enough to reach these leaves!

LORDLY LION

No one messes with the king of the jungle!

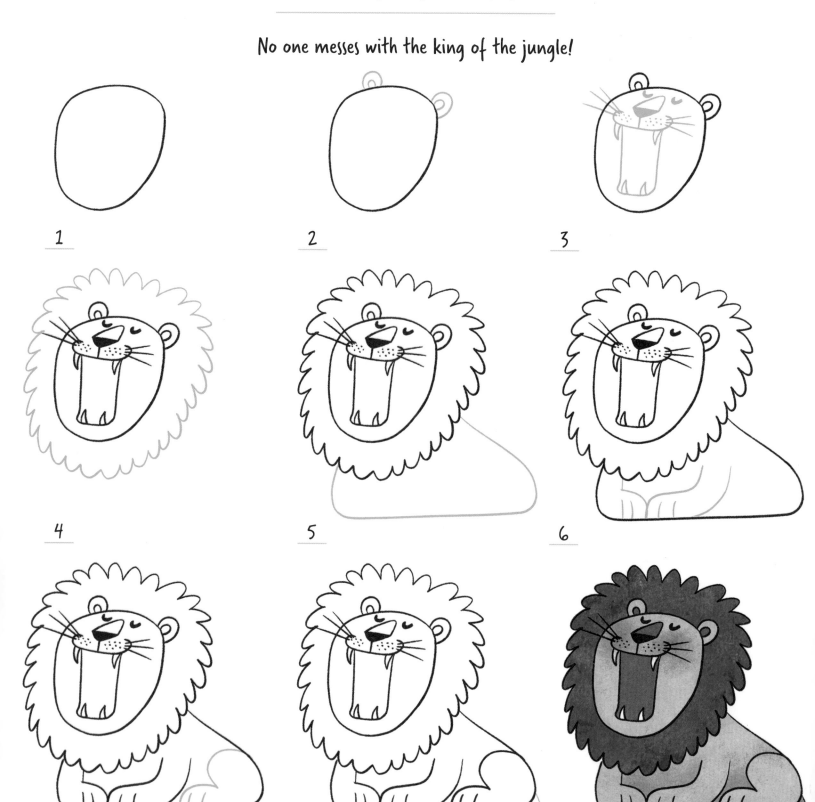

CUDDLY CUB

Now that you've drawn dad, it's time for the kids!

1

2

3

4

5

6

7

8

9

RUGGED RHINO

This tough-looking guy is not so tough to draw.

1

2

3

4

5

6

7

8

9

Imagine you're on a wild African safari. Draw yourself
and friends looking out of the safari truck at the wild rhinos.

AMAZING OSTRICH

The world's biggest bird is an impressive sight.

FANCY FLAMINGO

The pretty pink flamingo rests on one leg.

1

2

3

4

5

6

7

8

9

ZIPPY ZEBRA

Every zebra has a different striped pattern.

Finish the zebras that are missing their stripes, then add some more to the herd.

HAPPY HIPPO

The huge hippopotamus loves to wallow in water.

1

2

3

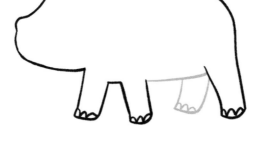

4

5

6

7

8

9

CRAZY CROCODILE

Sketch this croc, and make it snappy!

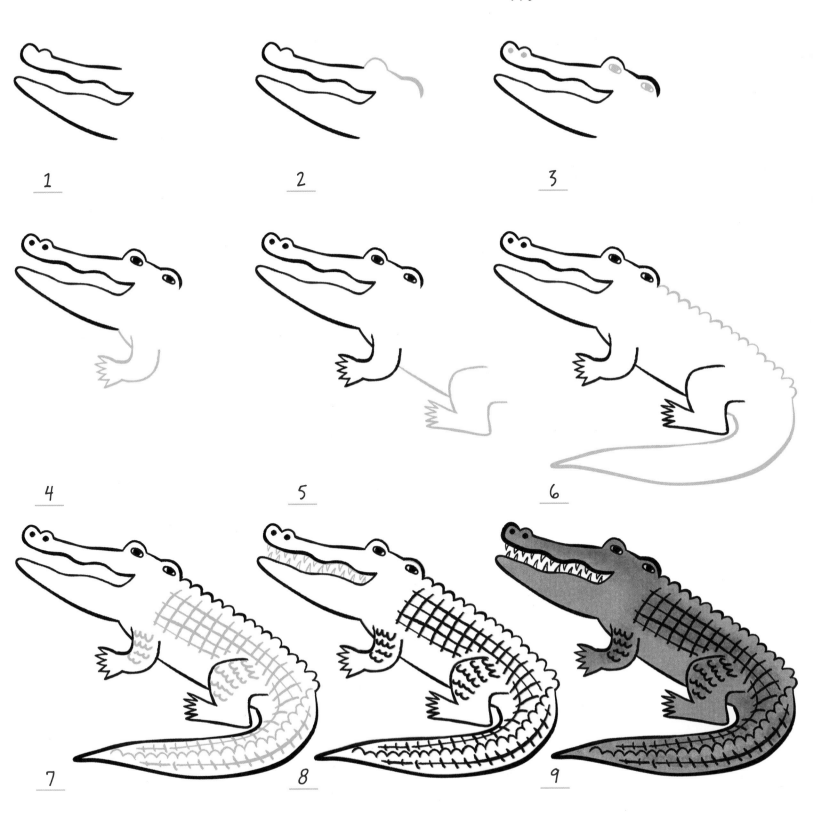

Using pages 46–47 to help you, add a family of hippos
and some crocodiles in and out of this watering hole.

TUSKY WARTHOG

This wild pig relative has fearsome tusks.

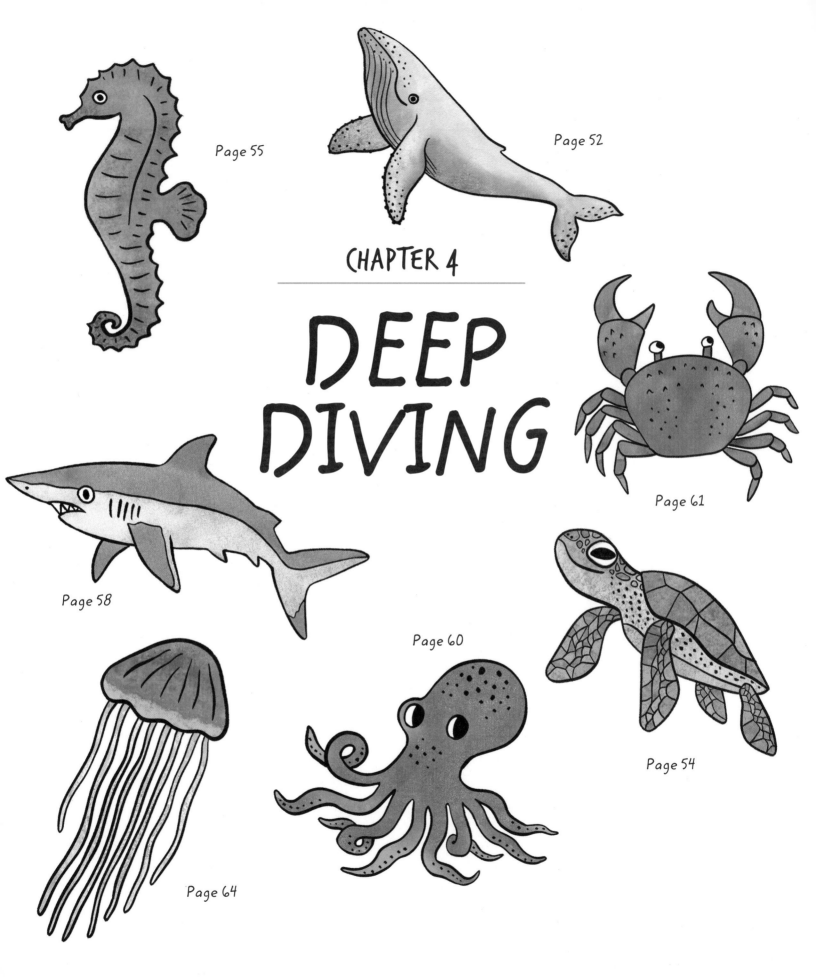

CHAPTER 4

DEEP DIVING

WONDERFUL WHALE

This humpback whale is a jolly giant of the ocean.

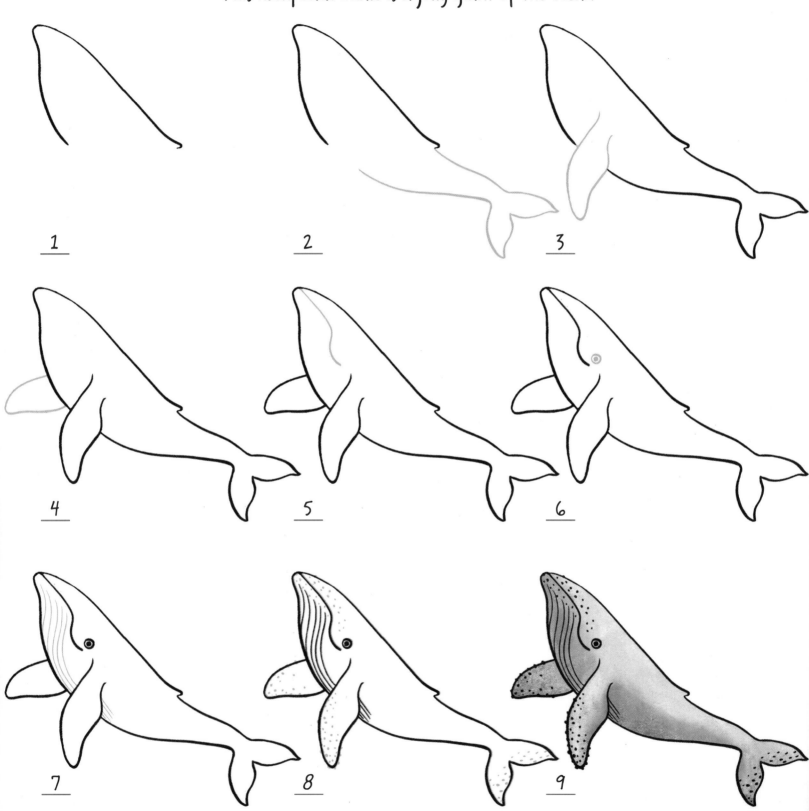

Draw a huge whale swimming beneath the waves.

TERRIFIC TURTLE

Turtles have feet that act like flippers underwater.

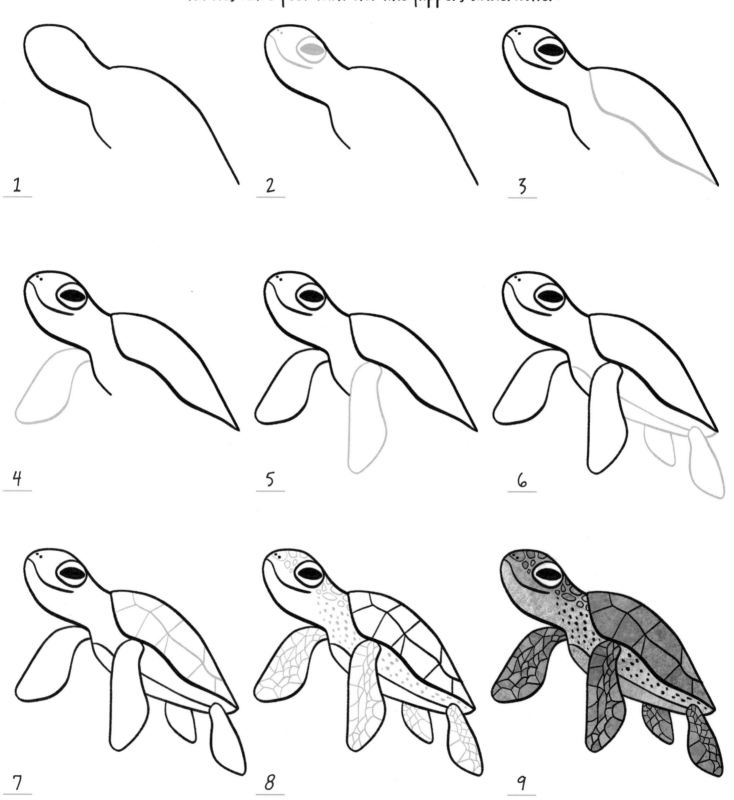

SPLENDID SEAHORSE

This tiny creature uses its tail to grip onto coral.

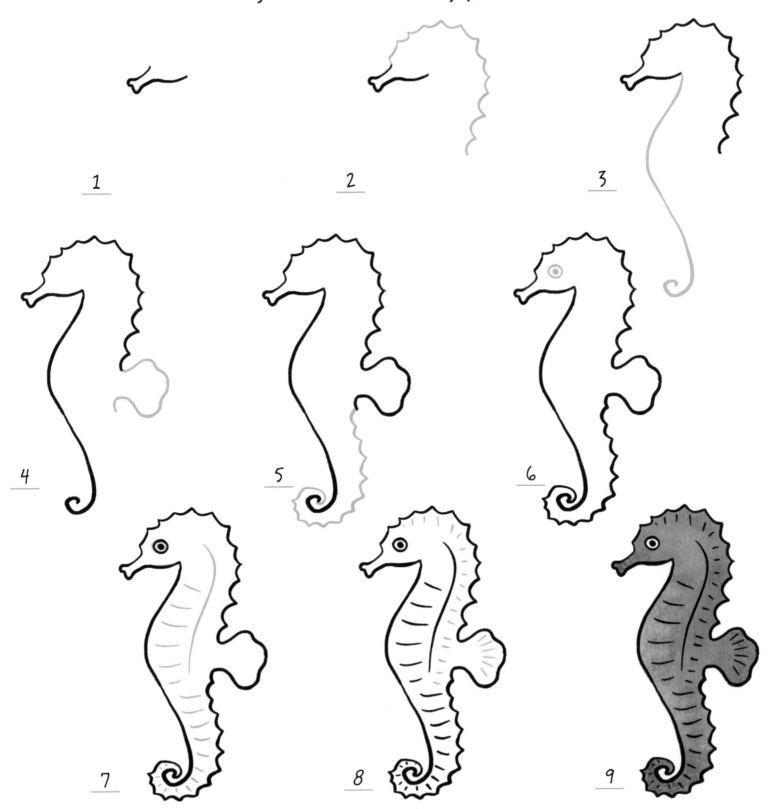

Invite some turtles and
seahorses to this cool coral reef.

Choose some of the coral below to add to the scene.

SNEAKY SHARK

This shark has bite. Don't let it chew your pencils!

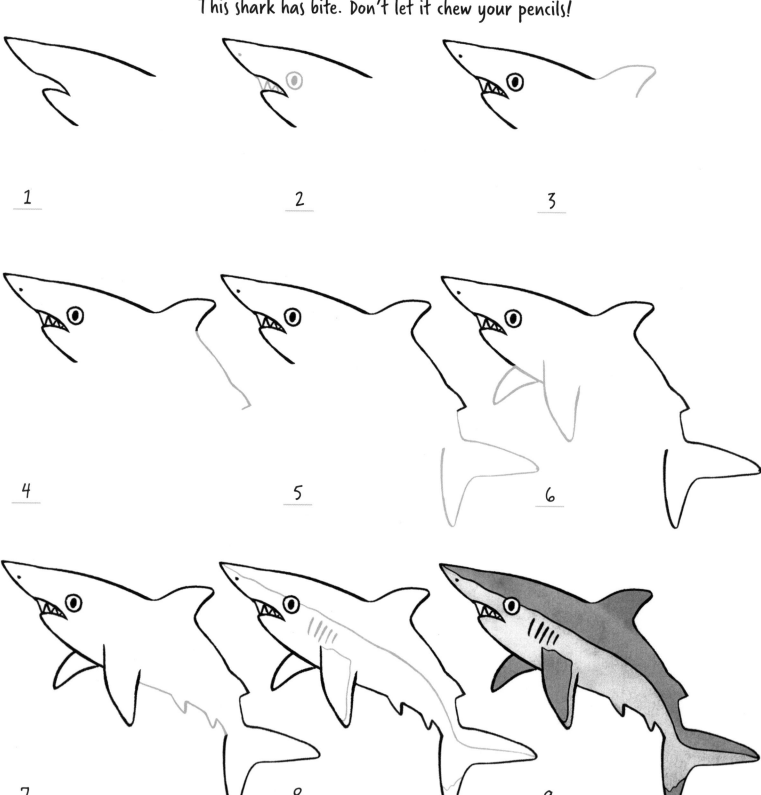

1

2

3

4

5

6

7

8

9

Sharks are known to patrol
this rusty wreck. Draw some in!

SLY OCTOPUS

This eight-limbed octopus can squeeze into a tight space.

SNAPPY CRAB

Crabs have five pairs of legs, with claws on the front pair.

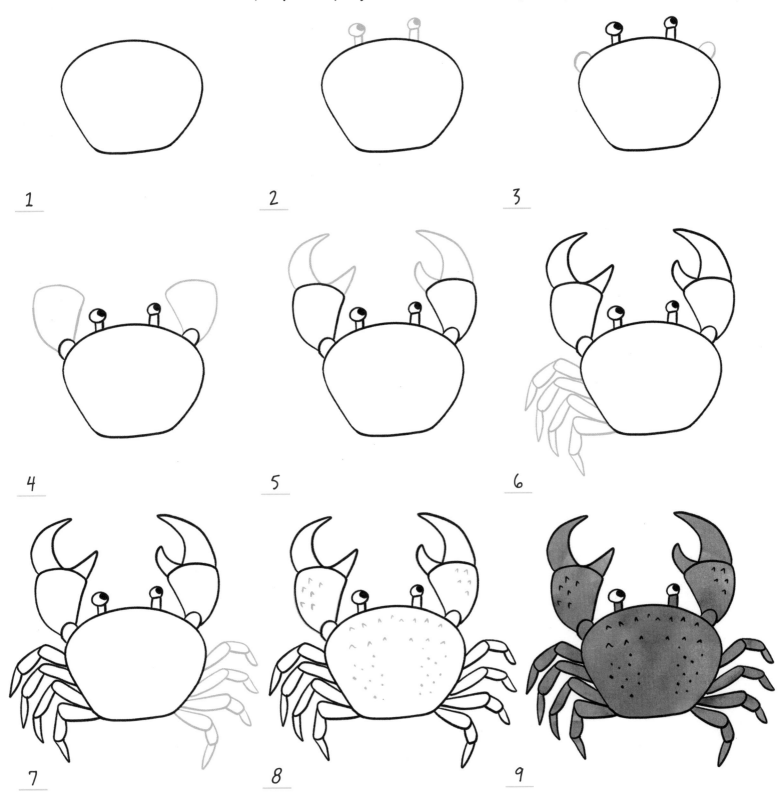

1

2

3

4

5

6

7

8

9

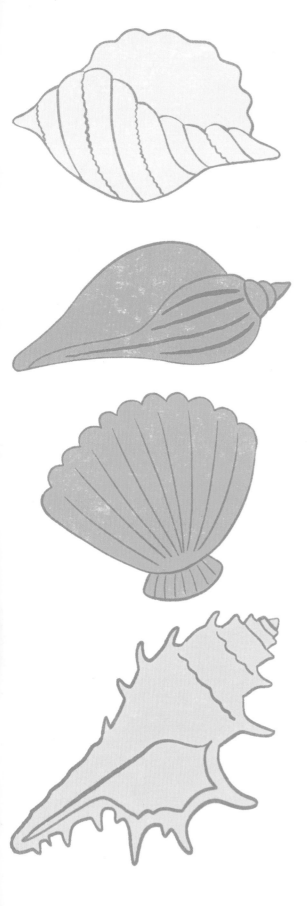

Here's a sandy seabed for your octopuses and crabs to call home.

Choose some shells to add to the sand.

WIGGLY JELLYFISH

The jellyfish has many tentacles but no brain, eyes, heart, or bones!

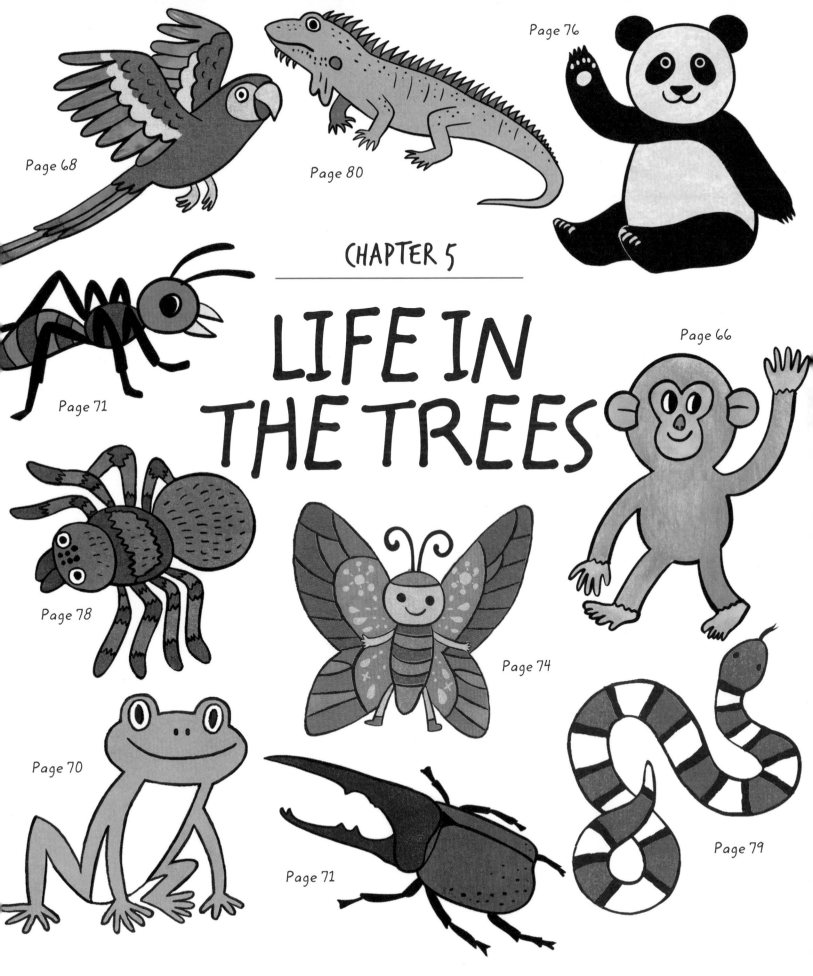

NAUGHTY CHIMP

Now that you're in the swing of things, try drawing a chimpanzee.

Chimps climb this tree to reach its tasty fruit.

RAINBOW MACAWS

The scarlet macaw has beautiful, bright feathers.

1

2

3

4

5

6

7

8

And here's a blue-and-yellow macaw, too!

The macaws fly high above the rain forest.

TREE FROG

The tiny tree frog spends most of its life above the ground.

JUNGLE BUGS

Meet two rain forest bugs—the stinging bullet ant and the Hercules beetle.

Add some tree frogs and bugs
to this rain forest scene.

BUTTERFLY BEAUTY

Try your hand at drawing this winged wonder.

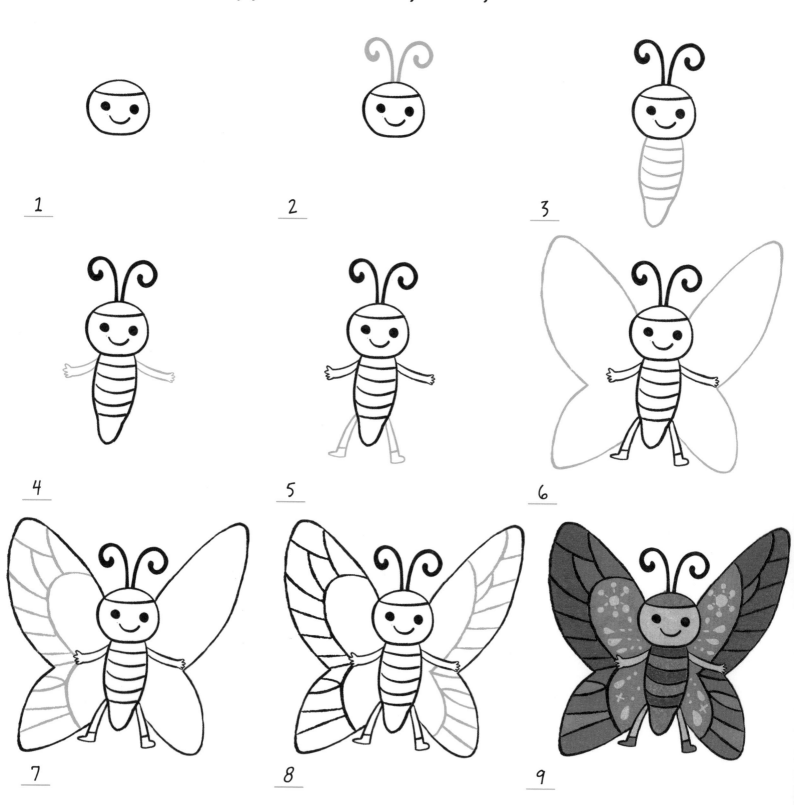

1

2

3

4

5

6

7

8

9

Complete the patterns on the butterflies' wings with bright and beautiful shades.

PATTERNED PANDA

This Chinese bear spends half its day chewing bamboo.

1

2

3

4

5

6

7

8

9

There's plenty of bamboo here to keep a pair of pandas happy.

TARANTULA

This big jungle spider is hairy, not scary!

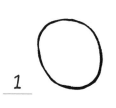
1

2

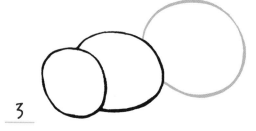
3

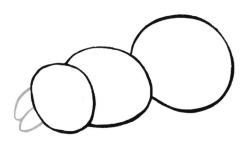
4

5

6

7

8

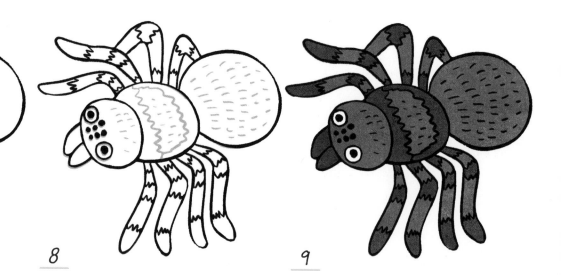
9

SCALY SNAKE

This slithery snake coils around tree branches.

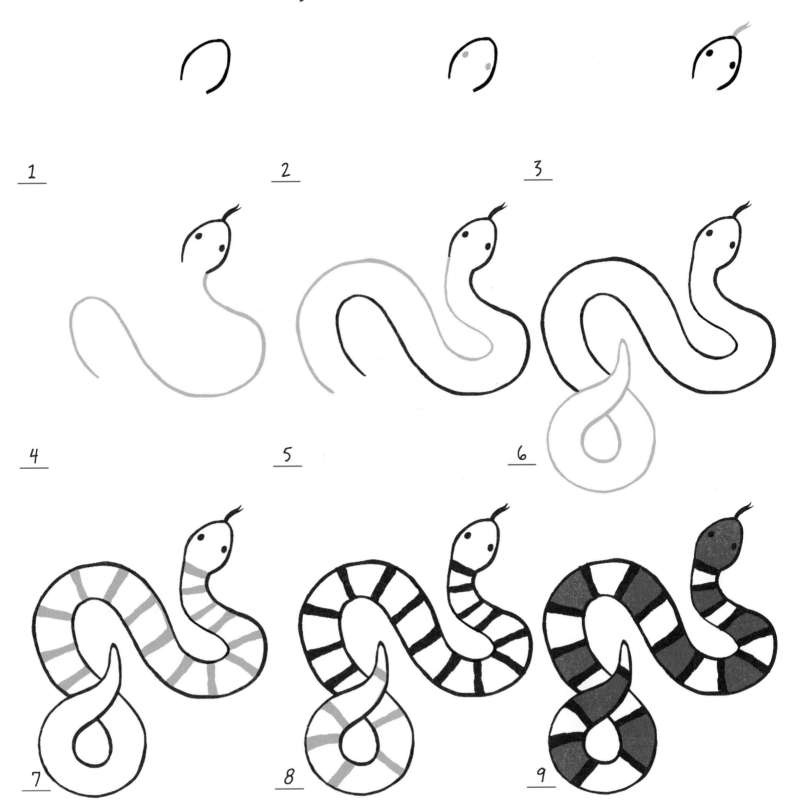

1

2

3

4

5

6

7

8

9

IDLE IGUANA

This large lizard has a row of pointed scales along its back.

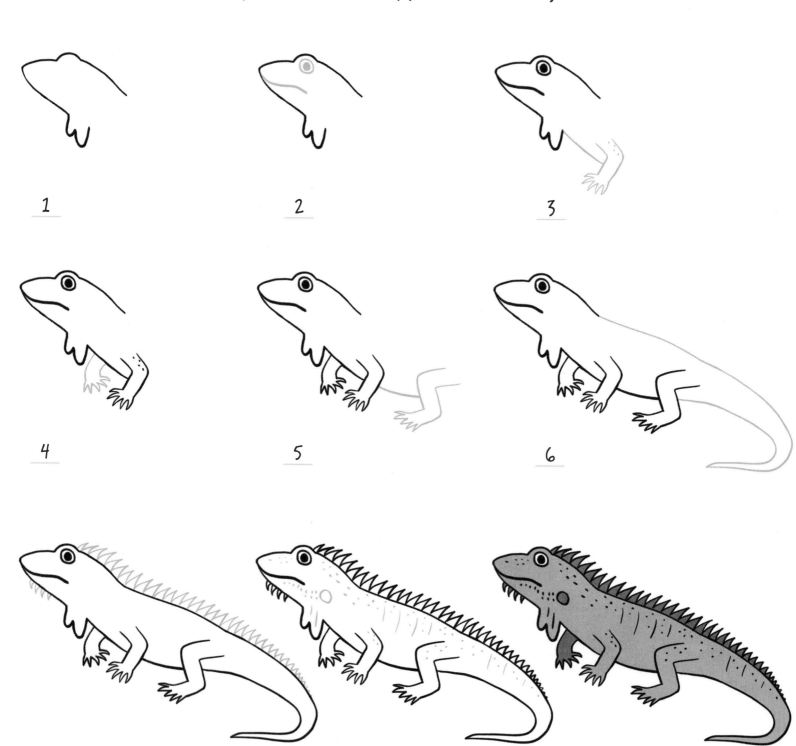

1

2

3

4

5

6

7

8

9

PERKY PENGUIN

This cute little guy will feel at home at the South Pole.

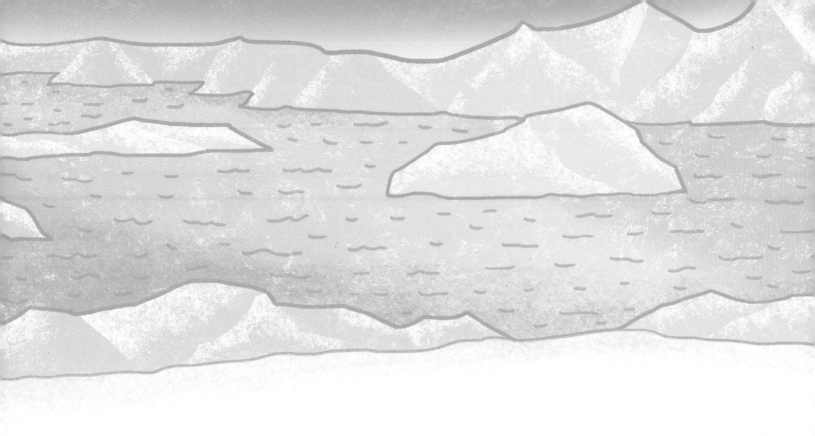

The penguins line up on the shore, ready to dive for fish.

WHISKERY WALRUS

This blubbery Arctic mammal has whiskers and long tusks.

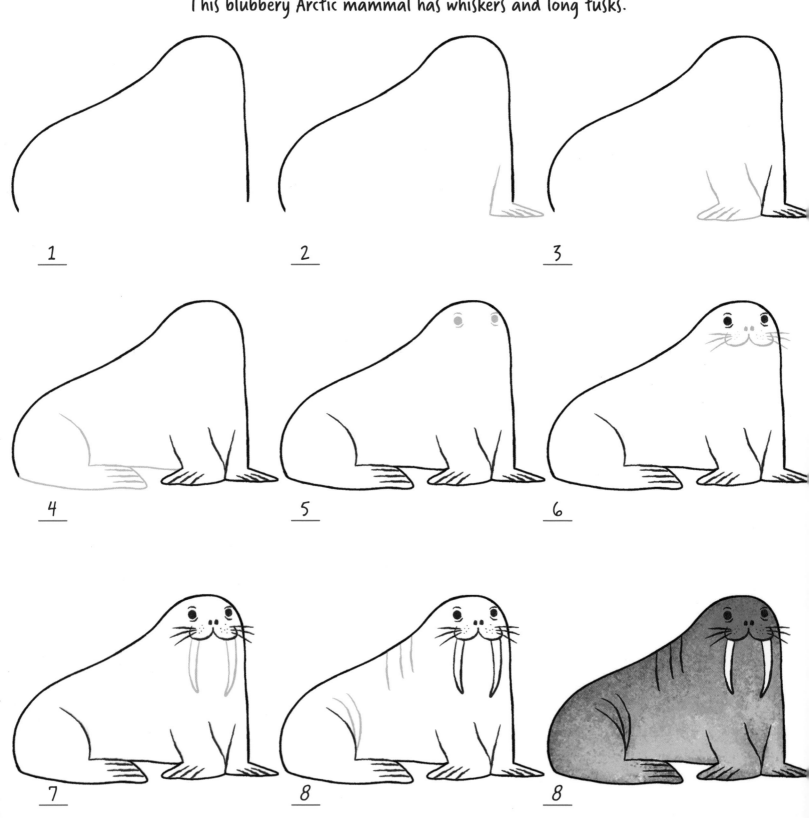

1

2

3

4

5

6

7

8

8

Time for the walruses to hit the beach for a lazy afternoon.

POLAR BEAR

The world's largest bear is as white as the snow.

Draw some polar bears exploring the sea ice.

AWESOME ALBATROSS

The albatross has the longest wingspan of any living bird.

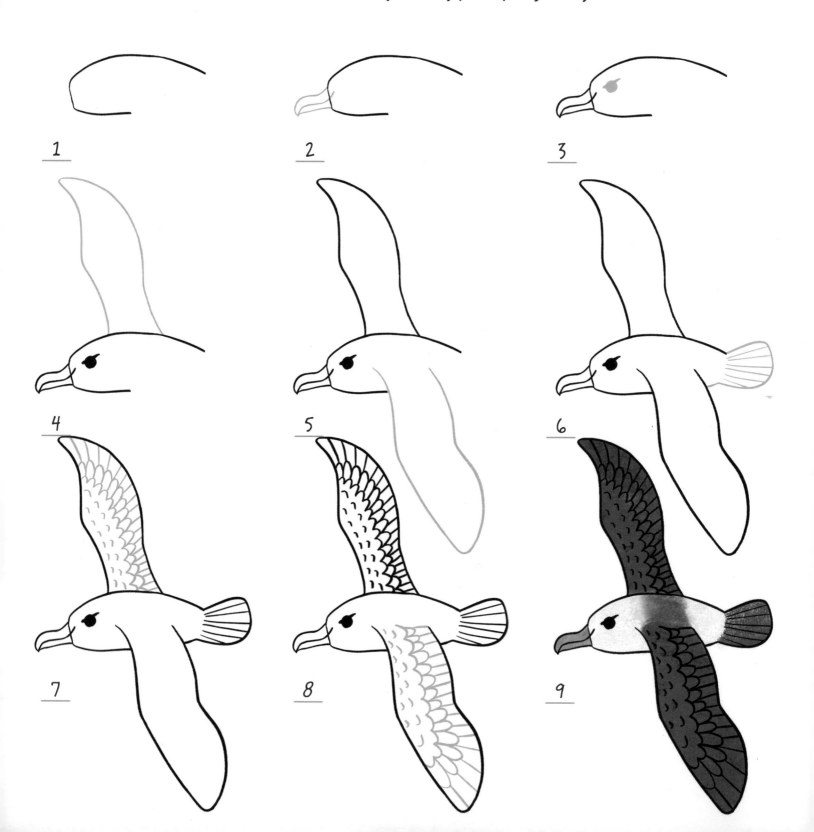

Add a hungry albatross looking for a tasty catch.

ROVING REINDEER

Reindeer, or caribou, grow new antlers every year.

1

2

3

4

5

6

Choose from different antler styles, or create your own!

7

Draw a happy herd of reindeer on this snowy mountain.

ARCTIC FOX

The Arctic fox has furry pads on its feet for walking on snow.

1

2

3

4

5

6

7

8

9

SNOWY OWL

This white owl has a sharp beak and talons.

Hide some snowy owls and Arctic foxes in this chilly scene.

PRETTY PUFFIN

The fish-eating puffin has a bright, patterned beak.

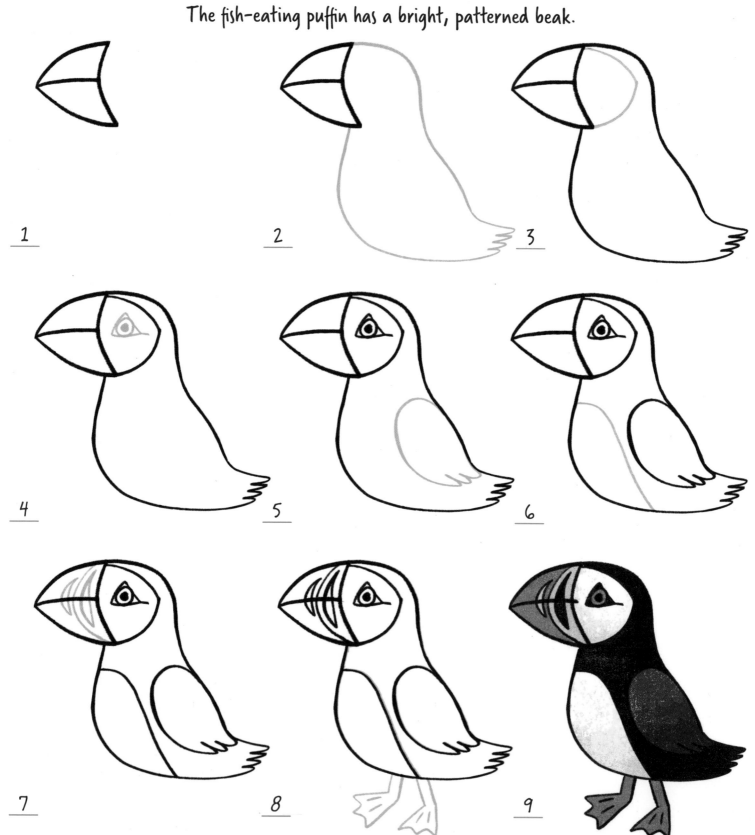